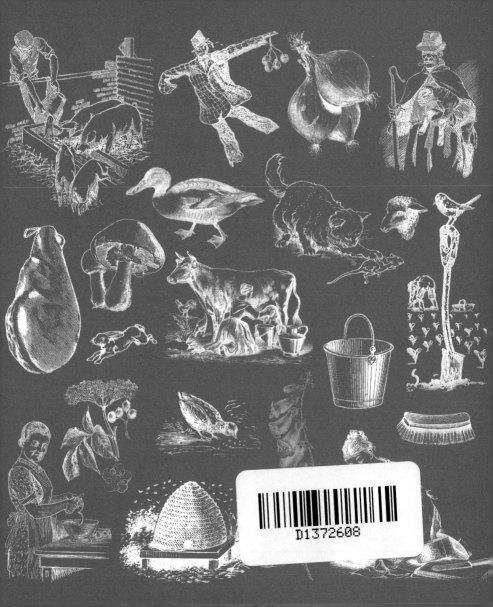

Tips from the
OLD COUNTRY FOLK

Elizabeth Drury

CONARI PRESS

First published in 2005 by Conari Press,
an imprint of Red Wheel/Weiser, LLC
York Beach, ME
With offices at:
368 Congress Street
Boston, MA 02210
www.redwheelweiser.com

Library of Congress Cataloging-in-Publication Data available upon request.

ISBN: 1-57324-218-7

Printed in Thailand

12 11 10 09 08 07 06 05
9 8 7 6 5 4 3 2 1

Contents

_____

"Place hive in good aier, set southly and warm,
And take in due season, wax, honey and swarm."
Thomas Tusser
1524?–80

Foreword

Once upon a time many of the country folk of Britain were smallholders. Like Old Macdonald of the song, they had a duck, a pig, a cow, a chicken, a horse, a sheep, and a dog and a cat (all of them making signature noises).

They grew fruit and vegetables, and a few flowers on either side of the path leading up to the door of their cottage. They foraged in the woods and fields and hedgerows to supply other of their needs. They captured wild animals for the pot. They made butter and cheese, pickles and pies. Their eggs really were "new-laid" and their mushrooms truly "dewy fresh".

Back in 1817 the Radical reformer William Cobbett said that it should be possible to provide most of the food for a family on a quarter of an acre of land. He wanted cottagers to be self-supporting and well supplied with food and clothes, for this, he believed, made a nation powerful and honoured in the world.

Some of his ideas seem a bit strange today. In "Cottage Economy" he railed against the drinking of tea. Anyone could see that tea rendered the body feeble and produced in men "a softness, an effeminacy, a seeking for the fire-side, a lurking in the bed, and, in short, all the characteristics of idleness".

Beer was the thing. The average family needed 274 gallons of it a year. Every labouring man should go to work on a breakfast of bread, bacon and beer, so he gave instructions on how to make them. He also advised on keeping livestock and proclaimed the importance of treating dumb animals with gentleness and feeding them with care.

Between the time of Cobbett and the present day came two world wars, during which people living in the country reverted to being subsistence producers. They grew potatoes and cabbages on all the available land and were encouraged to search for provisions in the countryside; they kept a pig and few chickens; they made use of everything that the bee produces; rabbit featured interminably on the menu.

Here are some of the notions and hints that over the years have been familiar to smallholders and country folk generally – but not necessarily put into practice.

Old-time cottages and country folk

Hearth and home

Old cottages belong to the countryside. They seem just to have grown there like mushrooms, tinged and coloured by all the local influences of soil and climate.

They were built on the edge of woods and common land, beside lanes and streams, in hamlets and villages, and close to larger farmers' houses. Their occupants were the families of estate workers and farm labourers, blacksmiths (and other smiths) and rural craftsmen.

Besides being homes, they were often workplaces, for there were once thriving cottage industries.

"Behold the cot! Where thrives the industrious swain,
Source of his pride, his pleasure, and his gain."

The cheering blaze

"To have no fire, or a bad fire, to sit by, is a most dismal thing," wrote William Cobbett. "In such a state man and wife must be something out of the common way to be in good humour with each other."

A well-built fire is a most sympathetic companion. Dancing flames and a crackling fire mimic our laughter, its warmth comforting and sustaining.

Collecting brushwood and bringing home furze and faggots for the fire were never-ending occupations. The loppings of pollarded trees and leftover branches when hedges were re-laid were both good sources of supply.

Green wood carries about a third of its weight as water, which on the fire evaporates and helps to carry the heat away up the chimney. Generally speaking, close-grained smooth woods make better fuel than those in which the grain is open and rough.

Firewood

"Oak logs will warm you well, if they're old and dry.
Larch logs of pine will smell, but the sparks will fly.
Beech logs for Christmas time; yew logs heat well.
"Scotch" logs it is a crime for anyone to sell.
Birch logs will burn too fast; chestnut scarce at all.
Hawthorn logs are good to last, if you cut them in the fall.
Holly logs will burn like wax; you should burn them green.
Elm logs like smouldering flax, no flame to be seen.
Pear logs and apple logs, they will scent your room.
Cherry logs across the dogs smell like flowers in bloom.
But ash logs, all smooth and grey, burn them green or old.
Buy up all that come your way, they're worth their weight in
  gold."

Chimney care

Apart from sending small boys up the chimney to sweep it *à la* "Water Babies" – a practice discontinued in the mid-nineteenth century, at about the time Charles Kingsley wrote his book – the Victorians had some other ideas.

One was to throw a hen or a goose down it to flap the soot away with its wings. Another was to tie a bunch of holly half way along a length of rope, drop the rope down the chimney and, with one person standing atop and another in the fireplace, pull it up and down. In some country areas the men fired shot up their chimneys.

Burning empty tins (sardines, baked beans, etc.) on the fire until they are red was later said to be an excellent way of cleaning a chimney, but can this be true?

Fireside fun

On long winter evenings cottage folk might gather round the fire and tell stories, sing to the accompaniment of a pipe or a fiddle, or play games.

Conundrums used to be popular, and among the church-going generations many of the word-puzzles had a biblical theme.

Why was Ruth very rude to Boaz?
Because she pulled his ears and trod on his corn.

How many wives are you allowed by the Prayer Book?
Sixteen: fo(u)r better, 4 worse, 4 richer, 4 poorer.

What animal took most luggage into the ark and which the least?
The elephant, who had his trunk, while the fox and the cock had only a brush and a comb between them.

Making light of it

To take a candle to light the way to bed was, of necessity, the way it used to be. And within living memory.

Candles were made for the home or for selling. Tallow (melted-down animal fat) was used, or beeswax. The candles were formed in a mould or were made by dipping and dripping.

Rush-lights gave a poorer light. A soft rush was cut and put in water, then peeled leaving a length of the outside to support the inner pith. This was dried in the sun before being dipped in fat. A rush-light smelled terrible for the average five and a half hours that it took to burn down.

Home work

Lace-making, basket-making, spinning and weaving were among the cottage industries; patchwork, quilting, knitting and crochet, and rug-making were crafts practised in many homes.

Every scrap of material was saved, either for patching clothes or for patchwork. Old bed covers illustrate the history of frocks and curtains in a household.

Always work with fabrics of the same weight with patchwork, and always wash and iron them first. And remember that you can't cut it down. Make sure that the pieces will fit the size of the foundation piece, or lining, you have chosen.

Quilting was sometimes done in combination with patchwork, and with strips of different-coloured fabric. The stitches held the warmth-creating wadding in place and were arranged in decorative patterns. The wadding was an old blanket, or sheep's or cotton wool. (It's apparently a myth that thistledown was ever used.)

Rugs for the floor were made of wool or bits of rag drawn through canvas – even a piece of sacking.

13

Flawless floors

Doormats are very important for preventing mud and grit being walked into the house. A foot-scraper outside the door – especially the back door – is a good idea too. The tread of country shoes and boots might have been designed to offer unwanted muck a lift into the house.

A layer of thick brown paper laid on the floor, beneath the underlay, will help to stop rising damp reaching the carpet.

Linoleum is made from canvas thickly coated with a preparation of linseed oil and powdered cork. One way of cleaning linoleum suffering from the effects of age and wear is to rub into it a mixture of milk and turpentine, afterwards polishing it with a warm cloth. This should make it feel much better.

Follow the grain of the wood when scrubbing a wooden floor.

From time to time give rush matting a dose of water, administered from a watering can.

Wash stone floors with water and a little ammonia or washing soda. Using any kind of soap is a bad idea as it is absorbed by the stone and the floor will become slippery when it is damp. Use fuller's earth and oil of eucalyptus to remove stains.

Trad paints

To make limewash mix one part lime putty to one or two parts water, depending on how porous the surface is. Binders such as tallow or size can be added so that the paint doesn't flake off quite so easily. Brush the paint onto a previously wetted surface. Be careful not to let the limewash get onto you, and particularly not into your eyes, as quicklime is caustic and will burn. Once dried it has a more benign disposition.

Limewash is good for old, traditionally damp, cottages as the surface absorbs moisture and allows it to evaporate (rather than sticking around behind the paint, and creating bubbles and cracks).

Distemper contains finely powdered chalk mixed with a gelatine binder — rabbit's skin glue, for instance. It is the cheapest type of whitewash for cellars, stables and other outbuildings.

Especially with limewash, don't forget to wear a hat when painting the ceiling.

Dogs and cats

Canine and feline truths

Although in England it rains "cats and dogs" – the cat symbolic of a downpour and the dog of accompanying gusts of wind – I prefer to think of them in the reverse order. Dogs are, after all, Man's best friend.

Dogs and cats possess a natural antipathy to each other – just as do some people and peoples. A peace treaty should be signed at the birth of a dog or cat, or at the first encounter, if they are to share accommodation and the affection of their owner. They should never be left alone together until terms have been agreed and proper introductions made. Things could get bloody and noisy, otherwise.

They must learn to respect the differences and preferences of each other. They must learn not boast about being the favourite. They must not share a hairbrush or any other cosmetic tool.

Inherited skills

The ancestors of today's dogs were bred and trained to work for a living. Some were supposed to guard people, property and livestock; some pulled sledges or searched for people lost in the snow; others specialized in herding or retrieving. Their descendants may be required to do the same jobs. They may have little work experience but none the less inherit their forebears' talents and skills.

Don't be surprised when a pointer stops stock still and points at something, a greyhound chases and outpaces deer and hares, a dachshund thinks it's his business to deal with a badger, a collie to herd sheep without permission, a cairn to go ratting and a pug — well, to look antique and Chinese.

"Dogs bark as they are bred"

Introductions with dogs

People shouldn't stare at dogs. They really hate it.

When first acquainting yourself with a dog offer the back of your hand to its muzzle. A dog is tempted to snap at fingers but will only bother to sniff at the back of the hand. Once he accepts that first introduction he will probably allow a friendship to develop to the stroking stage.

Over-enthusiastic dogs, and dogs who want to give you the equivalent of a warm welcome, jump up and put their muddy feet on your nice clean clothes. The way to deal with this lack of consideration is to step gently on their back feet at the moment they leap.

Dogs should be made to sit for a moment when they come into a new place. They can then survey the situation calmly instead of tearing around hoping to find food or potential enemies. After a moment they can be allowed a tranquil voyage of discovery.

Personal hygiene

Lots of dogs, particularly country dogs, never have a bath and no-one is the worse for it. But sometimes it is absolutely necessary. Believe it or not, you can temporarily overwhelm the smell of something unspeakable that a dog has rolled in to increase his allure to others of his kind by bathing the offending part with tomato juice. In North America this is said to be an effective deodorant for even the smell of skunk, which is quite something.

When bathing a dog wash him from the tail forwards. As soon as you wet his head he will shake and involve you in the purification process. Rinse in reverse, starting with the head so as to clear the dog's eyes as quickly as possible.

In winter the use of yolk of egg in place of soap was advised. And dry shampooing – rubbing bran or talcum powder into the coat and brushing it out – was suggested as an alternative to bathing.

Fleas, etc.

Egg yolk was used in an old recipe for ridding a dog of fleas: egg and water with a teaspoonful of turpentine to each yolk, used as a wash. Should the tribe not be entirely dispersed, powdered camphor rubbed into the coat might prove effective, or a dousing with castor oil. Saturate the coat with the oil and leave for twelve hours, then cleanse the animal with yolk of egg and water. A small dog will require a pound of castor oil; a large dog such as a Newfoundland, four or five pounds.

A particular drill was recommended for the application of Persian Insect Destroying Powder. Dust the dog well with the powder and put him into a strong canvas bag in which some of the powder has been shaken about. Leave his head protruding from the bag and put over it a linen rag with holes for his nose and eyes. Lay the bundle on the ground and let him tumble around as much as he likes – the more the better. In an hour or two let him out of the bag and scrub his coat with a stiff brush.

Ticks can be loosened for removal by hand by dosing them with ether, turpentine or alcohol on a piece of cotton wool. Whisky and gin work just as well.

 "Sleep with a dog and rise with fleas"

A dog's dinner

Teach puppies to lap by pushing their heads into the food for a second. They ought then to lick the food off their muzzles and look for more.

Dogs suffering from a cold or catarrh often lose their appetite because they can't smell their food properly. Strong-smelling food, such as ripe cheese, will often tempt them to resume eating. Dogs are gourmets (as well as gourmands) but in general are much more impressed by the smell of their dinner than the taste.

Vegetables should be on the menu three times a week – potatoes (but not the parings, which should be kept for the pig), cabbage, parsnips and beetroots (but not their skins). Nettles and turnip tops are excellent for a dog's coat, and windfall apples too.

To prepare a dog for a show dose him three times a day for two weeks with cod-liver oil and a tonic made up from two grains of powdered rhubarb, half a grain of quinine and five grains of extract of dandelion.

"Dogs wag their tails not so much to you as your bread"

Do and don't

Do give a dog a good name or he might despise you.

Give every dog his own bowl, preferably with his name on it.

If you own a large dog that you can't control do stay on good terms with your solicitor by paying his last bill.

Don't get involved in the debate as to whether a dog looks like his master, or vice versa. It is like the one about which came first, the chicken or the egg.

Don't criticize dogs for:

- Turning round three times before lying down. Their forebears, living wild in prairies and meadows, had to trample down long grass before making themselves comfortable.
- Barking at night. They had to keep in touch with the rest of the pack.
- Burying bones in the flower bed. They needed to store food against times of famine. (It's annoying that they have to dig them up to check supplies from time to time.)

Remember that a bore is a person who talks about his own dog – or cat – and won't listen when you talk about yours.

Cat facts (not fat cats)

A hungry cat makes a good trap.

Country cats and town cats – alley cats – have slightly different responsibilities and rights. The duty of your country cat in keeping down rodents is more important for here they do more than steal the odd bit of cheese. They should be rewarded for bringing home their "kill" for your approval, disagreeable though it is. It is extremely unfortunate – and inevitable – that they should expect the same reception for bringing home small birds that do no harm to anything or anybody. They are also apt to stalk and bring home creatures simply to torment and play with. It is in their nature.

Cats should be fed just enough to keep them healthy but not so much that they give up their day job, searching the hedgerows, and night job, locked up in a barn or the kitchen.

Cats definitely don't like the smell of peppermint oil, oranges and lemons. They think twice about walking on any surface that is wet. They do like the smell of cat mint but find themselves in competition with bees.

A yawning cat is a happy cat.

"In a cat's eyes, all things belong to cats"

Indoor cats

Houses in the country are apt to be draughty, to say the least. Taking up an agreeable position at the back of the Aga is their right, provided they agree not to dip their toes into a saucepan of warming milk. It is also legitimate for them to push aside pot plants on window sills so that they can watch what's going on outside from a comfortable place.

Put bicarbonate of soda in the drinking water of cats who insist on treating your house as if it were the out of doors. This reduces the smell of urine.

To get rid of stains on the carpet treat it with an equal quantity of white wine vinegar and water, then rinse with water and leave to dry.

To put off fleas feed your cat with something that makes it smell of yeast. Fleas don't like biting animals that taste of yeast.

A cat sleeping with its paws over its nose is a sign of bad weather to come.

A cat must sharpen his claws and stretch his muscles. If nothing else is available he will dig his claws into the furniture, so provide him with a rough-barked log or something like that. Put it somewhere where you won't fall over it or you will curse the cat.

Fowl

Residents of the poultry yard

The fowl is a most efficient machine for converting second-class vegetable protein and waste animal protein into first-class animal protein that is excellent for human consumption.

On keeping chickens

"Wherever there is a cottage family living on potatoes or better fare, and grass growing anywhere near them, it would be worth while to nail up a little pent-house, and make nests of clean straw, and go in for a speculation in eggs and chickens." That was the opinion of the sounded-headed Harriet Martineau.

The chicken run

A bantam or two (of ethnic Indian origin) add style to the chicken run.

Except in winter, chickens should be let out of their house for half an hour or so before giving them their breakfast so as to give them a good appetite.

When giving them greenstuff, such as cabbage or lettuce, it's best to hang it up so that they can reach up and pick at it. This gives them a gymnastic occupation, which they sorely need in confined runs. (Greens give a characteristic orange colour to the yolks of their eggs.)

A dustbath is their idea of heaven. As well as providing the feel-good factor, it suffocates and destroys unwelcome lodgers.

 Poultry in confinement require a supply of grit for without it they are unable to digest or grind their food. Grit is to poultry what teeth are to human beings. A moping chicken is often one that has been deprived of such matter. Crushed oyster shells are best, but cockle or mussel shells would do, or as a last resort old mortar.

"Children and chicken must always be picking"

The knowledge

A broody hen gives notice that she intends to try for a family by fluffing up her feathers and sticking up her tail feathers in a most self-important manner. A hen sitting on her eggs is one of the cosiest sights in the world and her clucking one of the most contented sounds. (She's a very good foster mother, too, and will happily take on pheasants' or ducks' eggs if asked.)

The chicks most likely to fatten well are the first born of the brood and those with the shortest legs.

If by accident a chicken, or any other fowl, breaks a leg, set the bone using a split twig of elder as a splint.

One cockerel per flock is quite enough and even one may make you enemies in the neighbourhood. He usually crows three times during the night as the quality of light changes. You can try shutting him up in a really dark coop so that he doesn't see the sun rise, but he usually finds out anyway.

Before deciding to keep chickens consider ducks. They are less liable to disease, quick growers and infinitely more likeable.

The aforementioned duck

"The manners and actions of the duck, whether upon land or water, are curious and pleasant to contemplate," wrote Bonington Moubray, Esq., in his practical treatise on domestic poultry of 1816. "Their regular afternoon parade and march in line, the elder drakes and ducks in front, from the pond homewards, is a beautiful country spectacle, to be enjoyed by those, who have a relish for the charms of simple nature."

The notion that the varieties of duck that have the bill bending upwards lay the greatest number of eggs is nothing more than an old wives' tale.

Most helpfully, ducks eat slugs but it's not good for young ducks to have too many. It's bad for their health.

Never allow a duckling near water until it's at least a month old. Before that it's too young to swim.

"If there's ice in November that will bear a duck,
There'll be nothing but slush and muck"

Goose and gander

Geese are undemanding creatures. They are quite content with a diet of grass and do not expect anything special in the way of housing. They are also quite prepared to be driven (by foot) to wherever you want them to be.

If geese wander off during the day, or even take to the air, you can lure them home in the evening with a handful of corn.

Goose feathers used to be collected from a cottager's flock five times a year for bedding and cushions.

If geese eggs are hatched by a hen they must be turned by hand each day as they are too heavy for a hen to do it by herself.

The gander is an exemplary father, very protective of his young.

Geese have at least one bad habit. They have a trick of pulling out corn from a stack by the straw to eat the grain from the ear. This may make the stack so lopsided that it eventually collapses. But they are very good at clearing the windfalls in an orchard.

Goose grease anointed on the neck is a country remedy for a sore throat.

Is every goose silly?

OLD COUNTRY FOLK

The turkey bird

When the Spanish first saw turkeys in America they described them as the "peacocks of the Indies". Their association with Christmas dinner was already established in England by the reign of Henry VII.

The hen turkey is the most ladylike of birds. She looks so well-bred, so gracefully nonchalant as she pecks indifferently at grass-seeds as she passes.

The best-bred turkeys come from Norfolk, the blokes weighing up to forty pounds.

On the whole turkeys have an antipathy to the colour red.

If, after hatching, the chicks seem particularly helpless and confused, take them into the kitchen and give them a small pill of ground pepper, bread and port. Letting them put their feet into a spoonful of whisky warms them up if they are cold.

Guinea fowl

The design of the head of a guinea fowl is one of Nature's most imaginative. The large red wattles and conspicuous red nostrils are set off by very pale blue skin; the feathers that stick up along the back of the neck are a fashion extra.

They are among the noisiest members of farmyard society, specializing in a chuckle. The two-syllable cry of the female – "Come back, come back" – is like the creaking of an old greaseless axle.

There is an old country saying, "A farm that has guinea fowl has no rats". Perhaps rats don't like the noise they make or perhaps guinea fowl are such good scavengers that there's nothing left for the rats.

Guinea fowl would sleep in trees from choice. Prohibit them from going to bed in a tree near the house. They do a lot of exclaiming and scaremongering on moonlit nights. If you want their eggs it is best to encourage them to sleep with the hens in the hen house.

They are not, by the way, related to guinea pigs

Animal husbandry
Cows, pigs and the rest of them

To husband is to make careful use of resources (which could be done by either a husband or a wife, one would think). In relation to animals it means getting everything you can from them – milk, meat, wool, leather, manure – and it involves looking after them in return; it means livestock farming and here we're really talking about cows and pigs and goats and sheep. These are the featherless animals that a smallholder would almost certainly have kept in days gone by. They certainly earned their keep if they were treated right.

Cows

Cobbett on cows

Anyone who doesn't know how to make a shed for a cow from poles, wattles, rushes, furze, heather and a cooper's chips is unfit to keep one, said Cobbett – or a cat, for some reason.

It's a good idea to turn her out into a field or onto common land from time to time. If that isn't on the cards, "have her led by a string, two or three times a week, which may be done by a child only five years old, to graze, or pick, along the sides of roads and lanes".

The house cow

A good dairy cow is very feminine to look at and in all her mannerisms. Her skin is soft, she has a pretty face and a slender neck, and good calf-bearing hips. She is gentle and sweet-natured.

Let loose in an orchard, cows have a disconcerting habit of pulling off apples from the trees and getting them stuck in their throats. This is no laughing matter. It may be a laughing matter if they get tipsy from eating windfalls that are turning themselves into cider.

If you want to stop a cow fidgeting when she's being milked hold up her tail from near the base.

The pox

A disease from which cows used to suffer was cowpox, which could be communicated to whoever milked the diseased cow. The upside of this was that the milkperson ("bovine attendant") who caught cowpox seemed to be immune to smallpox. Hence the notion that milkmaids had good complexions (because their faces were not scarred by the disfiguring effects of smallpox) and hence Jenner's discovery of vaccination.

Bullish

Bulls are generally quite quietly behaved until they are two. After that they have only one thing on their minds and are not to be trusted. A bull is obviously happiest when he is in female company.  If he has to be confined for safety reasons he can sometimes be appeased by putting an in-calf cow with him in his stall.

"A bull should be not only one of a good sort, but also a good sort of bull"

Pigs

The value of pigs

Pigs are capable of a strong attachment to their owners – and vice versa – but no country person keeps a pig from motives of pure benevolence.

Every part of the pig is of value: the bristles for brushes, the skin for saddles, gloves and fine leather wares, the entrails for sausage skins – and that's not counting the meat. No wonder it used to be more common for a villager or labourer, in passing a cottage, to ask after the pig rather than the wife.

They are useful, too, for predicting a storm. They become agitated and run about squealing and collect straw in their mouths, taking it to a place of shelter for their warmth and protection.

"When pigs carry sticks, the clouds will play tricks; when they lie in the mud, no fears of a flood"

How to choose a pig

A healthy pig, and a good buy, is one that is alert and curious —
even, with good reason, suspicious. Only elephants have a more
knowing look in their eyes.

Cross-breeds are usually more energetic and grow more
quickly than pure breeds

Points of porcine excellence

Head	Small, high at the forehead; short and sharp in the snout and curving slightly upwards; eyes animated and lively; thin, sharp, upright ears; the jowl, or cheek, deep and full
Neck	Thick and deep, arching gracefully from the back of the head and merging gradually into a broad breast
Body	Deep, round, well-barrelled, with an ample chest, broad loins and a straight, broad back
Tail	Slender
Hams	Round, full and well developed
Limbs	Fine-boned with clean, small joints
Hoofs	Small and compact, with a straight bearing upon the ground
Skin	Soft and thin and of a bright pink colour

Stys and troughs

It is usual to condemn the domestic hog as a filthy brute while in fact everything depends on the trouble taken by the carer. Notice how he delights in clean straw on the floor of his home, luxuriating in it with evident pleasure, his twinkling little eyes and low grunt expressing feelings of contentment. (His fondness for wallowing in the mire is to provide his skin with protection against sunburn and the attacks of winged persecutors.)

Make sure that the pigsty has a forecourt, facing south and with walls that are not so high as to keep out the sun. It is important for pigs to do some sunbathing.

On the matter of troughs, the master pig generally puts his foot in it while he is feeding to prevent others coming near until he has finished. He is only trying to assert his male dominance and authority. But for reasons of household economy he mustn't deprive everyone else. The trough must be long enough for all the inhabitants of the sty.

A pig's dinner

The elasticity of a pig's appetite is legendary. In a wild state he is a consumer of roots and he rootles for them, causing unsightly damage to the verdure in so doing. A ring used to be put into his nose to make this activity painful. He is also partial to the odd reptile and insect.

In confinement he samples everything placed before him, animal, vegetable and mineral. He crunches up coals and cinders, and a good deal of earth as he searches for food. In fact these may be necessary to his digestion, so don't go to the trouble of washing turnips and mangolds before offering them to him.

Acorn-fed pork is said to be especially delicious. According to that ancient guru Pliny, acorns of the holm oak (ilex) make a pig sleek, but tuck him up and narrow him, turning him out eventually, however, a weighty parcel of sound, lean meat. Acorns of the common oak (quercus) fatten a pig well, but the meat is flabby. Beech masts make a pig feel jolly, his flesh capital to cook and easy to digest.

Pig moving

Getting a pig to move house or take a lift to market is one of the most difficult things to do. It is almost impossible to deal with the travel arrangements of more than one at a time.

Put a bucket over the pig's head while another person grabs hold of the tail. Then use a rope to make a harness that goes around the head and again around the belly.

And finally

A contented pig fattens well. Scrub his back with a whisk of straw or a scrubbing brush.

Early mornings and evenings are good times to commune with him, to discuss the state of the world and other matters. Bored animals never do well. Listen and watch for any sign that he is in any way out of sorts and act immediately. Tit-bits break up the monotony of his day and give him something to play with and think about.

"Unless your bacon you would mar, kill not your pig without the R", goes the saying. The months without an R are hot months and the meat will spoil.

"Pigs grunt about everything and nothing"

Goats

What you need to know about goats

Some people are partial to goat's milk, as it is rich and sweet, but goats are mischievous and unpredictable creatures. In the first place, she-goats hardly ever permit a stranger to milk them, and are apt to refuse to give their milk even to people they know well. When they think they are getting the kind of care and attention they deserve goats will deliver about four pints of milk a day.

They have a reputation for head-butting when you are least expecting an act of violence, but, using tact, this can be converted into a gentle nudge, an indication that they are expecting some sign of affection from you.

They are brilliant jumpers and it is advisable to tether a goat rather than expect it to be confined within an ordinary hedge or fence.

The inconstancy of a goat's disposition is illustrated by the irregularity of its actions. It walks, stops short, runs, leaps, approaches and retires, hides and draws attention to itself, and then flies off as if activated by mere caprice. Its behaviour is no less than eccentric.

And another thing

- Nanny goats are apt to be lonely without friends, so it's better to keep two. This could mean that you have milk all the year round.
- They like to eat short grass, with two meals a day of hay, oats, bran and maize meal, with a little linseed oil to keep their beards and coats in good condition during the winter. However, they are not fussy feeders and cases of eating disorders are unknown. They are opportunists. They will eat thistles and will make a hearty meal of paper – brown or white, printed on or not.
- As a treat, they like acorns and hedge clippings.
- They get bored quite easily and like to be taken for a walk.
- The best way of controlling a goat in a temper is to catch hold of his beard.
- Their hair was once much in demand for the wigs worn by church dignitaries and lawyers.
- Their skin, too, has its uses.

Sheep
Sheepish

Can you tell them from the goats?

"Of the sheep is cast away nothing," goes the saying. Mutton fat used to be made into ointment for chapped hands and chilblains, and to make boots and shoes waterproof. Children would wear a pair of old stockings dipped in mutton tallow over their shoes in snowy weather.

If you're thinking of planting an orchard so that your sheep can graze picturesquely beneath the blossom in Spring, remember to buy standard trees to give the sheep room to stand.

Sheep seem to cough more than most people. The roots of Good King Henry are supposed to be a good cure.

Mutton calendar
"Hot on Sunday
Cold on Monday
Hashed on Tuesday
Minced on Wednesday
Curried Thursday
Broth on Friday
Cottage pie Saturday."

By hook or by crook

Shepherds attach a metal hook to a stick to make a crook while talented ones carve a ram's horn to form the hook or handle. One way of making a crook is to find a tree that has obligingly grown a fork. By cutting just below the fork, and leaving one of the branches long as the shank and cutting the other short as the hook, a natural, organic crook is made. Another way is to train a tree to make a gently curving hook by bending down a lesser branch and binding it to a main branch.

Crooks with small hooks are designed to catch a sheep by the leg; larger ones are for catching them round the neck.

The saying "By hook or by crook" probably refers to the manorial custom of permitting tenants to extract as much firewood as could be reached with a shepherd's crook.

Rabbits

Rabbiting on

Country folk often used to keep a few rabbits in the backyard. They were bred for their fur, for meat, for wool, and sometimes as pets and for showing. The best breeds for eating were said to be the New Zealand White and the Californian rabbit, which grew up quickly and were ready for the pot in about eight weeks. The best wool comes from the Angora.

Hutches can be made out of wooden boxes with door-posts and doors added. If you build one specially you can give it a tarpaulin roof. Ideally, there should be an exercise yard or outdoor run, though the Angora is such an unadventurous rabbit that it can be left on a lawn provided there are no foxes or other natural enemies such as dogs around.

For mating the doe is taken to the buck's hutch, never the reverse, or the doe may turn on the buck. An adult doe that has not bred for a year or more may become a shy breeder. A good plan is to leave her for a day or two in a hutch previously occupied by a buck. She is then more likely to mate when tried the next day. (This was Ministry of Agriculture advice.)

You can tell that the mating has been successful if the doe is seen carrying straw from her bedding in her mouth to make a nest. She plucks fur from her breast to make it nice and warm.

Rabbits live on greens, but they must be kept off evergreens, such as box and ivy, and also acacia, laburnum and snowberry. Other plants that are poison to them are wild arum, bluebell, buttercup, corn cockle, celandine, dog's mercury, foxglove, fool's parsley, hemlock, henbane, meadow saffron, poppy, the various nightshades and  toadflax. That still leaves quite a choice. They particularly like plaintain, groundsel and dandelions. The greens should be fresh and not frosted.

They musn't be given potato and mangold tops and unripe mangolds either, but ripe mangolds and swedes are fine. Corn, bran, hay and household scraps (including tea-leaves and fruit-peelings) are offered by most rabbit keepers.

Horses

An equine postscript

A horse is not, of course, farmed but is used to living alongside the cow et al. For stable read "tractor shed" since tractors now do the work of horses.

The heavier, stronger breeds still come in useful for getting timber out of a wood where tractors fear to drive. Horsepower (five hundred and fifty foot-pounds per second) is to this day used as a unit of measurement of force. The word was coined by the inventor James Watt.

A horseshoe is an emblem of good luck. The prongs must point upwards to stop the luck falling out. Nelson had a horseshoe nailed to the mast of "Victory".

Never change the name of a horse. It's unlucky and it will annoy him.

Inhaling a horse's breath was said to be a cure for whooping cough, while a hair taken from a horse's forelock and eaten with bread and butter was said to be a cure for worms.

A horse's eyes will tell you much about his disposition; they should be fairly large, full and clear, with a kindly, intelligent expression. A small eye with a sullen look is a sign of bad temper.

Fur, feather and fin

To eat or not to eat

The wild things

All about us, in the air, in woods and fields, on common land, in streams, ponds and rivers, alternative ways of life are being led. About some of our country neighbours we know — and see — very little. This is particularly the case with the ones that are extremely small, the ones that either run like crazy or freeze when they hear someone coming, the ones that wear camouflage and the ones that live it up at night.

We capture game for the pot; we capture vermin (a superior form of pest) because they interfere with the way we live and farm. Most creatures in the wild don't fall into either category. They go about their business without our paying any attention to them — or they to us.

All freshwater fish caught in British waters are edible but not all are worth eating; some, like the bream, have too many bones to be bothered with and a minnow is on the small side.

Game

Deer and hares are game. Grouse, black game and capercaillie are game birds, so are pheasant, partridge, snipe and woodcock. Trout, salmon, char and grayling are game fish. Carp, perch, bream, tench, dace, roach, rudd, chub, barbel and pike are – rather unkindly – described as "coarse fish".

Fish is best to eat when it is fresh but game birds and venison need to be hung for several days (the length of time depending on the weather) before the meat becomes flavourful and tender. Game birds that swim (eg wild duck) are traditionally hung by their feet and those that fly by their necks.

(If you forget and leave them to hang for too long freshen them up with a dousing of vinegar and water.)

The rules of game birds

Since the mid-nineteenth century a licence has been needed for taking and trading in game.

The "close season" is when, for several months of the year, game must be allowed to breed unmolested.

It is forbidden to take game birds and hares on Sundays and on Christmas Day and *between* the following dates:

Grouse: 10th December and 12th August

Black game: 10th December and 20th August (1st September in Somerset, Devon and New Forest)

Capercaillie: 31st January and 1st October

Pheasant: 1st February and 1st October

Partridge: 1st February and 1st September

Snipe: 31st January and 12th August (1st September in Northern Ireland)

Woodcock: 31st January and 1st October (1st September in Scotland)

At times of the year when shooting is permitted remember Commander Beaufoy's advice to his son:

"Never, never let your gun
Pointed be at any one.
That it may unloaded be,
Matters not the least to me.

When a hedge or fence you cross
Though of time it cause a loss,
From your gun the cartridge take
For the greater safety's sake.

If 'twixt you and neighbouring
    gun
Birds may fly or beasts
    may run,
Let this maxim e'er be
    thine,
FOLLOW NOT ACROSS THE LINE."

Deer

Deer of the British Isles are the red deer, who live mainly in the Highlands but also in the Lake District and on Exmoor, fallow deer, which ornament the parks of country houses, and roe deer, which choose Scotland and wooded parts of England. They are the most stately of Britain's natives .

Roe and fallow deer are supposed to have their being in the wild but like to let themselves into the garden and eat the leaves and buds of plants. Roses they treat as if grown specially for them. They are repelled by the smell of scented soap, garlic, rotten egg, mothballs and human hair; some gardeners tie little muslin bags containing hair to their roses.

You can tell if deer have been about by their foorprints. Deer tracks are long and narrow and in two halves of the same size.

The antlers of deer – hartshorn – was in the past the principal source of ammonia; the bones, together with calves' feet, were the source of gelatine.

Wild rabbits

Wild rabbits are edible vermin. They breed up to seven times a year and produce an average of eight young each time. Peter or any unnamed rabbit will help himself to the choicest vegetables in the kitchen garden, under the very nose of the gardener, while a single family can devastate a whole plantation of young trees.

An old way of protecting trees was to paint each one with an infusion of tobacco mixed with enough clay to make it stick to the bark. Up to three feet from the ground should be treated as this is the height a full-grown rabbit can reach standing on its hind legs.

In the garden repel rabbits in the traditional way by sprinkling wood ash, crushed limestone, ground black pepper or even talcum powder on the soil. They dislike onions, garlic and marigolds, and are fearful of mulches containing human and dog hair. Being timid, rabbits are easily frightened by strange noises. Put an empty bottle up to its neck in the ground and they will be afraid of the sound of the wind whistling across its top.

Snaring rabbits is a poacher's trick.

"If three dogs chase a rabbit or a hare they can't kill it"

And hares

Hares count as game – ground game.

The ordinary brown hare is prepared to live almost anywhere in England. It can run at up to thirty-five miles an hour.

It's perfectly normal to see them leaping around and behaving like a "March hare" in April as well as March. They sometimes stand on their hind legs and box, which is also normal

You can tell a leveret by the size and softness of its youthful ears and pads, and the sharpness of its teeth. Leveret meat is, of course, tastier than the meat of an old hare.

A traditional English dish is jugged hare, cooked in an earthenware jug or deep stew-pot with oatmeal, apple and lemon, mushrooms, herbs and red wine.

A hare's foot, suitably washed and dried, and covered at the bone end, used to be found on ladies' dressing-tables. It was used for applying face powder and rouge.

"If the hare wears a thick coat in October, lay in a good stock of fuel"

Off the menu

It is many years – in fact centuries – since Parson Woodforde wrote:

*"January 28th. We had for dinner a Calf's head, boiled Fowl and
Tongue, a Saddle of Mutton ro[a]sted on the side table, and a
fine Swan ro[a]sted with Current Jelly Sauce for the first course.
The second course a couple of Wild Fowl called Dun Fowls,
Larks, Blamange [sic], Tarts, etc, etc . . .
I never eat a bit of Swan before, and I think it good eating with
sweet sauce . . ."*

We don't eat swan or lark any more; nor do we eat blackbirds
baked in a pie, although recipes for rook pie were still included in
cookery books until quite recently.

Hedgehog was the food of gypsies. They covered them in clay
and baked them in their open fires. (The fat of a hedgehog applied
to the inside of the ear, was said to be a cure for deafness.)

Don't even think of eating fox, badger or any other rodent
unless you really fancy squirrel.

Fishing

"When the wind is in the east,
Then the fishes do bite the least;
When the wind is in the west,
Then the fishes do bite the best;
When the wind is in the north,
Then the fishes do come forth;
When the wind is in the south,
It blows the bait into the fish's mouth."

Old trout and young trout

All trout have spots (but don't seem to be bothered by them). Apart from that, they have regional accents in the form of differences in colour, size, shape. Trout from limestone streams are silver; trout from deep rivers are green.

A moderate, rippling breeze and a chequered sky are perfect conditions for fly-fishing for trout. It is said that on the River Otter in Devon the fish rise best in a snow-storm. A calm day, bright sunlight and water that is low and clear all work to the advantage of the fish in prolonging life.

Moderately rapid runs, pools with a current passing through them, eddies and water carrying a brisk ripple or curl are the most likely places to catch trout with a fly.

They may sometimes be caught by fishing with a worm. The best worms are dunghill worms, probably because of their peculiar pungent smell and red colour.

Tickling is a technique perfected by poachers. To tickle a trout you stand in shallow water and wait for the opportunity to take a fish unawares. When one comes close you gently touch its back and then slide your fingers underneath to lift it out.

"Fish are not caught with a bird call"

Salmon

Unlike humans, whose stages in the cycle of life are described by such wishy-washy terms as "toddler", "adolescent", "middle-aged" and "geriatric", the nomenclature of salmon is specific, though with variants relating to the river or geographical region. (The season for freshwater salmon fishing – for those lucky enough to have the rights – varies also.) The names usually used are:

Alevin Newly hatched, tadpole-like creature

Fry Aged two to six months and four inches long at most

Parr Aged one, two and three years and while living in the river; up to seven inches long

Smolt Fish that has swapped its golden and brown coat and donned a silver coat before going to sea; weighs about two ounces

Grilse On return from first trip to sea in the year that it leaves as a smolt; weighs up to ten pounds

Salmon Grown-up fish. Like chickens, the male is known as the "cock" and the female as the "hen".

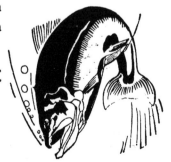

Cycle of life

Salmon usually spawn in the river in November or December and
go back to sea as *kelts*, or *spent fish*; they return as *clean fish*, fit
to eat. *Foul fish*, before spawning and while returning to sea as
kelts, are called *red fish*, if male, from their orange colour, or
black fish, if female, from their darker colour. After spawning the
males are called *kippers* and the females *shredders* or *baggits*.

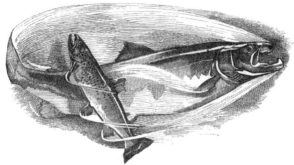

Grilse can be distinguished from *salmon* by the tail being forked
(as opposed to nearly square) and by the scales, which in the *grilse*
come off with the slightest pressure of the hand.

Fresh-run salmon, fresh from the sea, have lice on their
bodies, which drop off after a few hours and leave an unbecoming
mark for a day or two.

Fishing for salmon with a fly

Contain your excitement when you see a fish close to your fly and resist the temptation to strike early. Allow the fish to take and turn down with the fly. Then pull the line strongly so that the hook-point is pulled well over the barb of the fly.

Local knowledge as to where fish lie is more use to you than your best performance at casting. Generations of salmon frequent the same stone or at least the eddy behind it.

Don't give up if a fish rises to the fly but decides not to take. Try casting a little way upstream and bringing the fly gradually over the same spot. Or try changing the fly. But don't adopt either tactic too many times or it may get wise.

Keep flies in a box not a book so that they keep their crispness and resemble a living insect to the fish.

Lay up waders upside down (partly because they look scary the right way up).

Always wade using a stick as it is easy to slip. Drowning is an option if your waders fill with water.

"Never a fisherman there would be
if fish could hear as well as see"

In an English cottage garden
Pretty and pretty productive

Hollyhocks and sunflowers peering over the hedge, an abundance of roses, jasmine and honeysuckle around the door; snapdragons, nasturtiums, sweet william, marigolds and pinks seeded randomly, sweet peas and sweet-smelling lavender; herbs for cooking, rows of vegetables spaced neatly and economically, currant bushes and a few fruit trees: this is the very image of a cottage garden.

Mary Howitt wrote of the cottager's little patch of land:

"For though his garden plot is small,
Him doth it satisfy;
For there's no inch of all his ground
That does not fill his eye."

Many of the flowering plants would have had believed − if unbelievable − medicinal qualities. Powdered larkspur seed "kills lice in the head", for instance, and the juice of wallflowers was recommended for piles. Sweet william was said to "resist pestilence, strengthen the Heart, Liver and Stomach"; and "provoke lust" to boot.

Wild in the garden

Nature itself provides plants of almost unequalled charm for a garden. They may find their own way in. Besides the Sweet violet and the Welsh poppy, here are some of the native plants (with a selection of regional nicknames) that are quite capable of standing up for themselves:

Cuckoo Pint (Lords and Ladies, because starch
to stiffen ruffs was made from its roots)
Snowdrop (Candlemas bells, Fair maids of
February)
Wild daffodil (Lent lily, Daffydowndilly)
Primrose (Darling of April, Easter rose)
Cornflower (Bluebottle, Bachelor's buttons)
Wood anemone (Fairies' windflower, Granny's
nightcap)
Lily of the valley (Ladies' tears, Linen buttons)
Foxglove (Dragon's mouth, Deadmen's thimbles)
Snake's Head Fritillary (Bloody warrior,
Pheasant lily)
Meadow cranesbill (Blue basins, Granny's bonnets)
Harebell (Fairy bells, Witches' thimbles)

Fluttering by

Butterflies are noted sunbathers, so bear that in mind and choose a sunny place if you are planting to please them.

They have a list of their favourite plants, in general being attracted to purple, pink, yellow and white. Plant a mass of plants of one colour rather than one on its own.

Butterfly-friendly plants include asters, goldenrod, morning glory, sweet william, phlox, verbena, sunflowers and Michaelmas daisies and, especially, buddleia.

Butterflies in order of appearance

Brimstone (male before the sleepier female)
Peacock
Small tortoiseshell
Comma
Large tortoiseshell
Orange-tip
Holly blue
Red admiral
Painted lady

Gardening for the birds

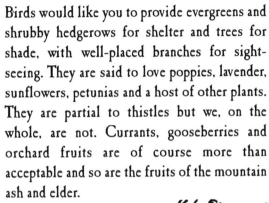

Birds would like you to provide evergreens and shrubby hedgerows for shelter and trees for shade, with well-placed branches for sight-seeing. They are said to love poppies, lavender, sunflowers, petunias and a host of other plants. They are partial to thistles but we, on the whole, are not. Currants, gooseberries and orchard fruits are of course more than acceptable and so are the fruits of the mountain ash and elder.

If you want to ingratiate yourself to birds leave herbaceous perennials to produce their seed before cutting them back in the autumn. Give them food on a table in the winter and enjoy watching their table manners.

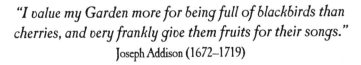

"I value my Garden more for being full of blackbirds than cherries, and very frankly give them fruits for their songs."
Joseph Addison (1672–1719)

The garden shed

This has a definitely masculine smell to it. It is the place for messing around with earth and creosote and oil, for fiddling with plant labels, twine, heavy and sharp implements and the odd machine such as the mower.

In winter, when there's less to do in the garden, you might even look after them like a caring owner. Some won't be used for a few months and deserve to be cleaned and oiled. A mixture of salt and lemon juice is good for cleaning them, and banana skins too.

Space small garden tools out on a board, draw round them and paint in their shapes. Then put in hooks from which they can hang and fix the board to the wall. It will be quite easy to see which tools have been borrowed or left in a tree or the flower bed.

When the handle on a spade breaks don't throw it away. Push the broken handle into the earth and use the top of the spade as a shoe-scraper.

And keep a perished hot-water bottle as a kneeler for weeding.

Vegetable matters

If you are chasing prizes, make a list of all the vegetables you have ever grown, putting them under two headings: those that were successful and those that weren't. Concentrate on the ones that did well. Either your ground suits them or you have a natural-born talent for growing them.

Marrows were once the most popular of the cottage vegetables. They needed their own space but were not averse to living and growing on a compost heap.

Vegetables that can be grown and eaten fresh all the year round are cabbages, carrots, onions and spinach beet.

You might thinking of planting scarlet-flowering runner beans or a row of Jerusalem artichokes to screen the rubbish heap.

"Plant the bean when the moon is light; plant potatoes when the moon is dark"

Scaring the living daylights

William Cobbett started out in life as a bird-scarer. Boys used to patrol the fields with a rattle or shaking a tin of stones, sometimes singing a song that began like this:

> *"You're harlock, you're harlock!*
> *O'er hedges and ditches*
> *You little brown witches!"*

An automatic terrorizing explosion set off at intervals with a cartridge does the trick, as do tins and silver paper loosely tied to sticks planted in the ground that clatter and reflect the light. Marauding birds that have been caught and tied to sticks put out a signal of revenge; rooks are supposed to be particularly frightened by the sight of one of their own kind hanged. Black threads stretched on pegs a few inches from the ground are another possibility

The most artistic answer is, of course, a scarecrow, dressed in old clothes and looking like a man. No old hat or jacket should be thrown away without first considering whether it could be used for a scarecrow – or for a guy on bonfire night.

Hedged in

Cut the stems (known in the business as "pleachers") at an angle so that they will bend but not break. Twist them diagonally between stakes to keep them in place and soon the bark will grow over the cut edges and make them firm.

Hawthorn (whitethorn) and blackthorn both have the character for a good hedge: they are easy of culture, quick to grow and capable of being trained in any direction. Haws, from the hawthorn, put in a bag and soaked in water all the winter and then sown in February or March, will come up the first year.

Hawthorn is linked to May Day ceremonies and was believed to protect people and livestock from evil influences and lightning; and witches too, who get tangled up in the prickles. Never bring May (hawthorn blossom) indoors, though. Because of its association with Christ's crown of thorns it is thought to bring death to the household.

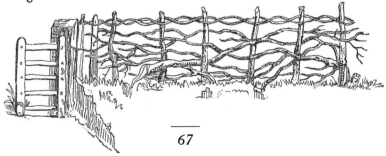

Getting a buzz

If Victorian water-colourists are to be believed, cottage gardens almost always had a beehive or two. Bees are renowned for their wisdom and their industry. They set a good example. Just as importantly, they work at pollinating the flowers and trees, at providing sustenance for the queen (whose only duty as sovereign is to lay eggs) and her subjects (drones, who are the aspiring husbands), so perpetuating their race; and at producing beeswax, and honey for people and bears.

Nature's provender at its sweetest is the honey from wild bees. Fortunate is the bee-fancier who comes upon a swarm and succeeds in enticing the queen and her entourage into private accommodation.

Early swarms have all the summer to collect and store nectar while late ones have hardly enough time to prepare for winter.

> *"A swarm of bees in May is worth a load of hay;*
> *A swarm of bees in July is hardly worth a fly."*

The bee at home

The medieval type of home and workhouse for bees was the straw skep. To make a skep all that was needed was a bundle of straw – preferably rye straw – some split bramble, the horn of a cow with the tip cut off and the bone of a goose or turkey with a hole in it. The straw was fed into the horn through the wider open end and emerged tightly packed from the narrower end, where it was bound round with the bramble. The straw rope thus formed was then coiled into a cone and sewn together in vertical stitches using the bone as a needle.

Skeps are not rainproof and they used to be seen taking shelter in a purpose-built wooden building or an alcove in a wall; others sported a modish conical straw hat or a hat made from an old earthenware pot.

Hives must be mice- and rat-proof so put tin around the legs of wooden hives or benches on which skeps are placed. To prevent ants making an ascent take a green stick, twist it into a ring to lie round the leg and cover it with tar.

Ideally, an apiary (where bees, not apes, are kept) should have a southerly aspect. Be careful that there are no bad smells nearby, such as proceed from a pigsty.

Travellers' tales

Bees will travel as far as two miles in search of nectar, making a "beeline" for lime trees, heather and clover. In the garden they love betony, borage and hebe, and it is worth planting crocuses and single arabis, which bloom in the early spring, and golden rod and Michaelmas daisies for the late autumn, as at those times the weather is not suitable for long flights.

The colour and flavour of honey varies according to where the bees have travelled to collect their nectar. Clover gives a light honey with a delicate flavour; heather honey is very dark and stiff with a strong flavour.

Bees versus flies

To make fly-paper take three parts honey, three parts resin, one part colza oil (any vegetable oil would do). Slowly heat the resin in a double saucepan (or a mixing bowl in a saucepan with water in the bottom) and when melted stir in the honey and oil. Spread the mixture on strips of paper.

Bee lore

- Bees must be kept informed of all important events in the household such as births, marriages and deaths, otherwise they may fly away or die.
- They must be told if you intend to move their hive and must never be transported over running water.
- A swarm of bees in the garden is a portent of prosperity.
- A bee landing on the hand foretells wealth.
- A bee flying into the house announces the arrival of a stranger.
- Dreaming of bees is lucky.
- On Christmas Eve bees hum the hundredth psalm in their hives.
- Bees will not tolerate argument or the use of foul language in their presence.
- The ashes of burned bees sprinkled over shoes is a cure for flat feet.
- Providing she is a virgin, a girl passing through a swarm of bees will not be stung.
- Honey should be kept in the dark. Bees, knowing this, work in the dark.

Fresh and wild

Hedgerow harvesting

Free for all

Of all the trees that are in the wood the holly may bear the crown, as the carol goes, but its berries, much prized by birds in winter time, are not recommended for normal human consumption. Nor are those of the mistletoe, another Christmas special.

But there are other berries that can easily be involved in the food and drink chain. Some of the trees and shrubs are self-seeded and have grown in the wild since birth; others have been planted in a particular place, for a particular reason, and then left to their own devices.

Then there are the various types of fungus and the plants, otherwise known as "wild flowers" and "weeds", that have nutritional and medicinal uses, and are there to be harvested for their flowers, leaves and roots.

Black and other berries

It's unlucky to eat blackberries after Michaelmas (29th September), when the Devil goes trampling on them. (Actually, they're past their prime by that date.) The best berries are the lowest of each cluster. They ripen first and are the largest and sweetest.

Country folk used to collect blackberries to put in buns instead of currants. They also collected them to sell for dye. The juice made navy blue and indigo. It's not surprising you get stained fingers from picking them.

You might be lucky enough to find wild raspberries, gooseberries, redcurrants or blackcurrants growing in the hedgerows. Treat them like their garden relations.

Look in woods and hedgerows too for haws from the hawthorn and berries from the rowan, both of which make excellent jellies to go with meat.

Bilberries are to be found – with difficulty – growing on heathland. Juniper also likes to grow there, and on chalk and limestone. The berries are a good accompaniment to game.

Most precious of all to discover, perhaps, is the wild strawberry. William Morris was an admirer of its looks and used the plant for one of his most popular designs. The taste is equally to be admired.

Nuts about nuts?

Remember, then.

Don't gather nuts on 14th September. This is the day the Devil goes nutting.

Brides used to be presented with a bag of nuts as a symbol of fruitfulness.

Nutcrack night is Hallowe'en, the time of year you would expect to enjoy the fruits of your nutting. ("Here we go gathering nuts in May" is obviously unrealistic: nuts should be "knots", as in knots of flowers for the May Day celebrations.)

Ignore acorns, which are only just fit for human consumption. During the Second World War they were roasted to make a poor substitute for coffee.

Home-bred almonds are hard to find nowadays. If you need a substitute – and have the patience – you can unpack the four small nuts from the prickly husks shed by the beech. But don't rely on a single tree. Beech only fruits every five or even ten years.

Or use peach kernels in place of almonds.

> *"Nuts are given to us, but we must crack them ourselves"*

Super-nuts

Walnuts are ripe when they fall, at the end of October or in November. If they reach the ground with their skins on put them in a sack and, with a person at each end, shake them together by tipping the sack backwards and forwards.

To pickle walnuts you must wear gloves as the stain of walnut juice is almost impossible to get off. You need to collect the nuts while they are still young and before the shells harden, in the early part of July. They should be soft enough for you to push a knitting needle through them.

For a hundred pickled walnuts add four pounds of salt to a gallon of water. Prick the skins first, then leave them in the brine for a week, until they are black. Let them dry and then confine them, topped up with vinegar, to a sealed jar. Black pepper, allspice, ginger, a few cloves, a little roughly pounded mace and a slice of horseradish may be added to the vinegar.

For trees that obstinately refuse to bear fruit there may be some truth in the saying,

> *"A woman, a steak and a walnut tree,*
> *the more you beat 'em, better they be"*

Browns

"Nut brown", as in browned by the sun; "chestnut", as for a brown-coated horse.

Horse chestnuts, aka conkers, are really no good to man or beast, but sweet chestnuts are another matter. Stamp the prickly husks on the ground to release the nuts. And don't forget to prick them before roasting in the ash of a fire – or bonfire – to prevent them detonating.

Wait till hazel nuts are beginning to fall before gathering them and leave them in their cases to store.

Gather pine cones in the autumn and heat them so the nuts can be shaken out. The nuts are particularly delicious roasted.

And greens

Young hawthorn leaves, picked and eaten on the way to school, are known to country children as "bread and cheese".

Living in hedges and ditches and on the verges of lanes are various plants whose leaves are acceptable as green vegetables. In the past they have been gathered by country folk either as a salad (spicing up garden lettuce, in the main) or to be cooked like spinach.

Greenstuff

	Salad	Cooked
Black mustard	*	
Chickweed	*	
Comfrey		*
Cow parsley	*	
Dandelion	*	*
Dead-nettle	*	
Fat hen		*
Good King Henry		*
Jack-by-the hedge	*	
Lady's smock	*	
Ramsons	*	
Sorrel	*	
Stinging nettle		*
Yarrow		*

Watery stuff

Culpeper recommended watercress soup as a remedy for headaches, consuming the "gross humours winter hath left behind".

It likes to grow near springs and in clear, cold water.

Before eating watercress as a salad wash it in salt water, pick it over and remove the part of the stem that has fine white rootlets and any yellow leaves. While it is waiting to be eaten put it in a bowl of water (never in the 'fridge).

Eat watercress for a good complexion. Bruising the leaves and rubbing them on the skin is good for the blemishes of adolescence.

Sea beet is actually called sea spinach by some people and can be treated in the same way.

Samphire grows in estuaries and salt marshes. It has to be picked at low tide and even then it's no easy matter as it enjoys twining round your legs and trying to trip you up. You can cook and eat it like asparagus or use young shoots as a salad vegetable.

Rootling around

The root of sea holly used to be made into jam and jelly, and, by boiling shavings of it in water with sugar and butter, a rather delicious kind of toffee.

Look for the hot-tempered horseradish plant in wet ground. The root is peeled and shredded for the traditional accompaniment to roast beef. (Mixed with animal fat, horseradish makes an excellent embrocation for sprains and rheumatism, by the way.)

Freckles are symptoms of someone who has spent time in the out of doors and, while adding to the charm of the childish complexion, not so much admired in grown-ups. Among the traditional methods of seeing them off was washing the face twice a day in a mixture of finely scraped horseradish that had been allowed to stand in buttermilk for some hours and then strained.

Beware the mandrake. Pulling up the forked root might mean you won't be able to have children – or it might not.

Liquid assets

Many a child has sipped rosehip syrup. The hips are cut up fine and boiled, and the liquid put to drip through gauze or linen as in jellymaking. Sugar is added at the end.

Elderflower cordial is a perennial favourite, while wine is made from elderflowers, cowslips, dandelions and various other wild things.

Wild cherries are used to flavour brandy and sloes from the blackthorn for slowly-made sloe gin.

Teas, or infusions, are made from lime blossom, the flowers and leaves of hyssop, blackberry leaves and heather, among other candidates.

Fritters

The flowers of the elder and the leaves of comfrey are excellent fried in batter.

Fungal fear and fare

There are only about twenty kinds of fungus that you might come across and really musn't eat. The properly named Death Cap is one. It has a faint but distinctly nauseous smell when mature. The greenish-tinged Yellow Cap is another and so is the Destroying Angel. The scarlet/orange character with white warts or patches that features in the lives of goblins and fairies is poisonous but not deadly. It's called the Fly Agaric.

Most mushrooms found in fields and woods are edible but don't excite the taste buds.

Things for mushroom fanciers to remember:
- Don't pick anything that you can't positively identify as being for the good of mankind.
- Be particularly suspicious of anything with white gills.
- Don't pick when they are wet.
- Be ageist and discriminate against any that are past their prime.
- Twist the stem to pick and then cut off the earthy part.
- Wipe rather than wash, and don't bother to peel them.
- Cut them in half before cooking to make sure others haven't got there first.
- Don't keep them for more than a day.

Delicatessence

Don't underestimate the puffball, which is around from July to November. Fried in butter, the slices are like white fish – without the fishy taste.

Fairy-ring champignons are the best for drying. They are quite easy to find in short grass between the months of April and December. Cut off their skinny legs and use a darning needle to thread them on a string, then hang them in a warm place such as an airing cupboard. Or kebab them and put the sticks across the bars of the oven.

Morels and ceps are good for drying, too. To reconstitute, boil them in liquid for about twenty minutes.

Oyster mushrooms, instead of raising their heads just above the ground (or growing below ground, like the rare and much-praised truffle), choose to live on dead or dying trees.

The field (snobbishly called "common") mushroom and the horse mushroom have quite a long season. They're around from July to November but not always available for selection.

Some wild remedies

Chickweed	For bruises make a poultice with the boiled leaves.
Clover	For nerves drink an infusion of the flowers and leaves. For flatulence, too.
Coltsfoot	For coughs drink as an infusion of the dried flowers or leaves.
Marsh mallow	For teething infants offer a root for sucking.
Periwinkle	For cramp tie around the affected part. (For heaven's sake don't eat it) For nose bleeds bruise the leaves and stop up the nostrils.
Plantain	For insect stings and bites and for wounds apply the crushed leaves. As a laxative, allow the seeds to swell in water and drink.
Tansy	To expel worms apply as a poultice to the tummy or drink the leaves or flowers as an infusion.

"A doubtful remedy is better than none"

Country fare
Making the best of it

Produce grown – or fattened – by the smallholder, and not intended for market, was prepared in the kitchen and preserved for the hungry gap that lasted from February to May; foraged foodstuffs as well.

Fruit was bottled and made into jam, vegetables pickled, meat salted and herbs dried.

Throughout the year bread was baked and milk converted into butter and cheese Then there were the home-made drinks, some sweet-natured and harmless, others powerfully sleep-inducing at best.

Bread, the staff (or stuff) of life

Cobbett despised the wife who did not bake her own bread. (He once saw a baker kneading bread with his bare feet in France and that may have had something to do with it.)

Kneading is the hard part. "The fists must go heartily into it. It must be rolled over, pressed out, folded up and pressed out again, until it be completely mixed into a stiff and tough dough."

A cottage loaf is in the shape of a small bun on top of a larger one. The dough, once it has proved (rested until it has risen), is twisted to form the two parts and patted down.

A cross is often marked with a knife on top of the dough, to keep out the Devil.

To tell if bread is done tap the loaf on its bottom. It should sound hollow and dry. Not yet done, the sound of the tap will be a thump, showing that there is still moisture in the middle.

To cut bread while it is still hot dip the knife in boiling water and quickly wipe it dry.

To refresh old, tired (stale, in other words) bread, moisten it and put it in a hot oven in a paper bag until crisp. Another way is to put the whole loaf in water for a couple of minutes and put it in a slow oven for up to an hour.

Milky ways

Morning's milk yields much more cream than milk from later in the day, so make butter from that and keep the rest for domestic use.

It used to be common practice to add a pinch of bicarbonate of soda to milk to stop it going off.

Pay attention to milk's neighbours in the larder (or 'fridge). Milk readily absorbs impurities.

Clotted cream – a peculiarity of Devon and Cornwall – is made by setting milk to warm (not boil) for a day and leaving it to cool during the night. The next morning scoop off the cream, which will be very thick.

The curds that Miss Muffet sat eating on her tuffet are the white globs that form when milk coagulates; in other words, curdles.

Whey is the liquid drained therefrom.

"That which will not be made butter must be made cheese"

Preserving and storing produce

Clamp potatoes by covering them with straw or bracken and beaten-down earth, or pile them up in the dark and cool of an outhouse or cellar and cover with sacking. Bury carrots and beetroot, unwashed, in light sand. Pumpkins and marrows can look after themselves on a shelf in a cool place or hung from a hook in nets.

Knot a group of socially compatible and dry onions together by their long stalks and plait the stalks round a piece of string. Then add to the original four with more onions, one by one, twisting their stalks round the string. Given half a chance onions go on growing after they have been harvested. To stop this, singe the roots with a red-hot poker.

Did you know that you can preserve a cabbage by cutting it with about two inches of stem, scooping out the pith as far down as a small knife will reach and suspending the cabbage upside down with string? You must fill up the stem with water every day.

Drying

Almost any food can be preserved by drying, in or on top of the oven, or in the sun. If the latter method is used – specially good for fruit and tomatoes – in strong sunlight spread the food out on a tray, preferably made of wood, and cover with cheese-cloth. Turn or stir every few hours and take the trays in at night. Prunes are simply dried plums or damsons.

Pick sweetcorn when young – or at least adolescent – boil the whole cob and then scrape the grains off before drying.

Preserved nasturtium seeds may be used in lieu of capers. Gather them from the flowers and dry them on paper for a few days. Then put them in a bottle and pour boiling vinegar over them. Cover once cooled. They will be fit to eat the following summer.

Herbs – wild or grown in the garden or in pots – should be gathered on a dry day just before they flower, immediately well washed and dried by hanging them up by their stems near the oven or in the sun. The leaves should then be pounded and sifted, put into stoppered bottles and labelled.

Salting

Salting is the next simplest method of preserving food. (Bay salt, which is mentioned in old recipes, is sea salt.)

"A couple of flitches of bacon are worth fifty thousand Methodist sermons and religious tracts," wrote William Cobbett. "The sight of them upon the rack tends more to keep a man from poaching and stealing than whole volumes of penal statutes, though assisted by the terrors of the hulks and gibbet."

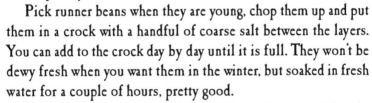

Silverside and tongue are cuts of beef that are frequently salted.

Pick runner beans when they are young, chop them up and put them in a crock with a handful of coarse salt between the layers. You can add to the crock day by day until it is full. They won't be dewy fresh when you want them in the winter, but soaked in fresh water for a couple of hours, pretty good.

To make mushroom essence sprinkle mushrooms with salt, leave for about eight hours, then mash and strain through butter muslin. Simmer until reduced by half. Bottle and cork tightly.

In a pickle

The most suitable candidates for pickling in vinegar are onions, gherkins, red cabbage, beetroot and walnuts.

Make and keep pickles only in wood, glass or stoneware. Other types of container, in combination with the vinegar (eg earthenware, because of the lead in the glaze) can be poisonous.

To spice (not spike) the vinegar ready for use add a teaspoonful of alum and a teacupful of salt to three gallons of vinegar, and pepper and perhaps ginger root, garlic, sliced horseradish, allspice and mustard seed. Heat this until it is almost bubbling and leave it to stand before straining.

If you want the vegetable to stay crisp use the vinegar cold.

Make sure the vinegar is topped up to cover the vegetables.

(With chutneys the vegetables and fruit are simmered in the spiced vinegar and sugar until they are reduced to a pulp and then bottled while still hot.)

All bottled up

The only vegetable fit for bottling is the tomato, but then a tomato is nearly a fruit.

The point about bottling (ie putting in a sealed jar) is that all the bad things are destroyed when fruit (or the one vegetable) and the water or syrup surrounding it is heated. You do this either by boiling the jar in a pan (covering it completely with water and using a lid) or putting it in the oven.

Dip the rubber rings in boiling water before you put on the lids – either screw tops or clip-down.

Don't let bottles knock together while they're hot or the glass might shatter.

Pears, unfortunately, go brown when they are bottled.

In a jam

Jam-making produces one of the sweetest smells. Fruit such as raspberries, red currants, plums and gooseberries have just the right amount of acidity and natural pectin to set well when boiled up with sugar and make excellent jam; strawberries need a little extra help.

The skill is to use firm, even slightly under-ripe fruit, soften it by heating and then add the sugar.

To reduce the froth that makes an appearance while the fruit is boiling, wipe the preserving pan round with butter beforehand.

To tell if the jam has boiled enough to set, test a drop when it has cooled to see if it wrinkles.

Cucumbers can be made into jam by boiling them with root ginger and sugar. The peeled and sliced cucumbers should first be allowed to stand under a weight of sugar equal to their own weight.

Yours cordially

As the name suggests, these are decidedly friendly drinks. Lemon barley water is specially recommended for invalids. Cut the rind of a lemon very thin and put this with two tablespoonfuls of barley into a jug, pour on two pints of boiling water and leave to stand overnight. The next day strain the liquid – which should be straw-coloured – and add sugar to sweeten.

Cherry-stalk tea, as it is called, made by pouring a cupful of boiling water over cherry stalks, is said to be a very cleansing drink first thing in the morning.

Country wines

Home-made wines are a way of using up surplus produce from the garden or wild produce gathered from the fields and hedgerows: parsnips, green gooseberries, rhubarb, cowslips, and dandelions and elderberries – even grapes. Over and above their hospitality value some wines have definite medicinal qualities, especially for promoting sleep (though perhaps not as effective in this respect as mead, which is made with honey).

To the vegetable matter is added sugar and soft water and, usually, yeast to speed up the fermentation process. (The yeast is normally spread on a piece of toast to float on the surface.) The sugar converts into alcohol. Once the liquid has fermented, turned into a cask and bunged securely, it is, officially, liquor.

You need patience if you make your own wine. It grows up slowly and really needs at least a year to mature.

Beer

Cobbett, as we know, insisted on the benefits of every cottager brewing his own beer

Wild hops, climbing all over hedgerows in the south of England, are perfectly suitable for home brewing. They should be somewhere between green and yellow in colour and have no brown marks; they should have a clammy feel and "a lively, pleasant smell".

Malt from plump barley is better than that from thin, light barley, we are told. The malt was made by wetting the grain and allowing it to sprout, then heating it and having it cracked in a mill.

Spring water is the best.

Cobbett recommended using a clothes basket for fishing the hops out of the strained wort.

Add the yeast and only pour the liquid into a cask (made of oak) once the brew has gone quiet.

Beer has been made using mangold wurzels instead of malt, and nettles.

"Turkey, carp, hops, pickerel and beer came into England all in one year (1532)"

Last-minute maxims

- Soup can be made with almost anything that is not sweet.

- To preserve the colour of green vegetables add a pinch of bicarbonate of soda as well as salt to the water and make sure that the water is boiling before you put in the vegetables. When the vegetables sink they are generally done enough, if the water has been kept constantly boiling.

- After chopping up parsley put it in the corner of a cloth and hold it for a moment under the cold tap, then squeeze it dry. It will be a brilliant green when you shake it out of the cloth.

- Wet seasons mean tender vegetable fibres; dry seasons mean tough, wiry stems. Old plants need cossetting and take far longer to tenderize than a frisky young thing in its first youth.

- Dipping a broken beetroot in flour before boiling it will prevent bleeding and retain the colour.

- Fruit should never be cooked in an aluminium pan. The acid dissolves the metal and metal really isn't good for you.